Schizophrenia

A Guide to the Symptoms, Management, and Treatment of Schizophrenia

Table of Contents

Introduction 1

Chapter 1: What is Schizophrenia? 4

Chapter 2: Signs and Symptoms 15

Chapter 3: How to Diagnose Schizophrenia 27

Chapter 4: Treatment 37

Chapter 5: How to Manage Schizophrenia 47

Chapter 6: How to Help a Loved One with Schizophrenia 54

Chapter 7: Alternative Therapies 64

Conclusion 73

Introduction

A lot of people are familiar with disorders like anxiety, depression, and OCD, but schizophrenia doesn't seem as widely understood as these disorders. While the public may have no problem recognizing or classifying schizophrenia as a mental illness, its familiarity, its symptoms, and its effects lack depth, which continues to cause excessive concern and the stigmatization of schizophrenic individuals. This results in hardships that only add to the suffering of the victims of schizophrenia, such as a lack of job prospects, relationships, and more.

The word "schizophrenia" has been around for about a century, but the illness itself was recognized much earlier. Certain types of depression, dementia, and other symptomatic behaviors related to schizophrenia were described long before it became a known disease. The term was coined back in 1910 by a psychiatrist, who combined two Greek words that translate to "split mind." While the reasoning behind this name revolved around disturbances of thoughts and feelings, many people mistakenly associated it with a split personality.

It is now actually becoming easier to distinguish schizophrenia from other disorders by understanding what it doesn't mean. A confusing intersection between split personality and schizophrenia may have clouded a lot of people's minds. Multiple personality disorder (MPD) is a much rarer mental condition than schizophrenia. One may actually be hard-pressed to find a psychiatrist who has dealt with individuals suffering from MPD. Nevertheless, the media's focus on a condition like split personality disorder has only harmed spreading awareness about schizophrenia.

Sigmund Freud and his school of thought have influenced and helped the evolution of the last century's psychiatry. It didn't take long for most psychiatrists in the U.S. to start recognizing schizophrenia and similar disorders as a form of an unconscious process of thought that is influenced by deep-rooted childhood experiences. Fortunately, the technological breakthroughs of the late 20th century have helped clear a lot of common misconceptions. Genetic research, neuroimaging, and medicinal advancements have paved the way for a more biological approach, compared to the previously presented model of Freud.

The current psychiatric view of schizophrenia primarily points to biological disorders that are present in the brain. Still, this doesn't necessarily mean that psychological elements like stress don't play a role in triggering the illness or at least making it worse. This is why schizophrenia treatment is often not as straightforward as many people would expect.

The most recent fact sheet by the World Health Organization states that there are around 20-million sufferers of schizophrenia, worldwide. Understanding how schizophrenia affects the human brain has been the goal of many psychiatrists for the past few decades. The good news is, that these psychiatrists have developed treatments and behavioral therapy techniques that can help sufferers or loved ones deal effectively with the disorder and manage it.

This book will delve deeper into the most recent findings of psychiatric research so that you may gain a clear understanding of what schizophrenia really is. We will also discuss the symptoms and signs of schizophrenia, as well as some of the common treatment methods that you may like to implement. From diagnosing it, to effectively helping a loved one manage it, this book will provide you with an informed overview of schizophrenia.

Chapter 1: What is Schizophrenia?

Considered a somewhat rare mental disorder, schizophrenia is a condition that mainly affects the brain. Perhaps the most common symptoms of this disorder are delusions, hallucinations, and decreased cognitive abilities. Because of these symptoms, some people associate schizophrenia with other mental disorders, namely dissociative identity disorder (DID). Although the signs might look similar to ordinary people, it is worth mentioning that schizophrenia and DID are completely different. Because of the hallucinations that schizophrenic patients usually experience, it may also look as though they suffer from a split personality.

Nonetheless, this is merely a misconception. While there is still a lot that psychiatrists do not know about this disorder, there has been a significant development when it comes to an understanding of its causes, symptoms, and potential management mechanisms. There has also been an improvement in how the public views schizophrenic patients. Despite the stigma that has previously surrounded this illness, with some allegations that it is closely linked to crime, people are now more inclined to deal with such a disorder the same way they would handle other mental illnesses, like depression.

History

It is important to have some historical background on schizophrenia to understand it properly. The term "schizophrenia" itself is relatively new, considering that it has been in use for roughly one hundred years. Does this mean that schizophrenia is a somewhat new mental disorder? Not at all. Although the term itself was not used to describe this mental condition, the disorder had been around long before the term was coined. Some psychologists believe that there is evidence that schizophrenia was a recognized mental illness in both ancient Greece and Egypt. However, patients suffering from the disorder were usually misdiagnosed either with bipolarity or dementia. In 1887, the salient psychiatrist Emil Kraepelin coined the term "dementia praecox," which means "early dementia," to differentiate between the two disorders. He thought that schizophrenia was a rare form of dementia that develops in fairly young patients instead of seniors, causing the deterioration of cognitive faculties. In terms of modern psychiatry, dementia and schizophrenia are distinctly different conditions. Still, Kraepelin's efforts paved the way for other psychiatrists to pay more attention to schizophrenia and try to find adequate terms to describe it.

In the early twentieth century, Eugen Bleuler, a prominent Swiss psychiatrist, came up with the term "schizophrenia" to describe the disorder. Schizophrenia is derived from two Greek words: "schizo" and "phrene." Since "schizo" means "split" and "phrene" means "mind," a lot of people think that the term refers to DID. Nevertheless, Bleuler used the term to refer to the jumbled thought process of schizophrenic patients, and not a real split in personality. Notably, Bleuler's classification of the symptoms tied to the illness is still used today, as he was the first psychiatrist to categorize them into two areas: positive and negative.

Is Schizophrenia Common?

Schizophrenia is not an uncommon mental disorder, but it is not as prevalent as other conditions like bipolar disorder or depression. It is estimated that about 20 million patients are suffering from this disorder worldwide. This may seem like a huge number, but considering that it affects only 1.2% of Americans, it is easy to see why schizophrenic patients often feel excluded. However, there have been many campaigns that raise awareness about the illness, its symptoms, and management plans to ensure that people know how to support their affected loved ones. Usually, the onset of the illness happens when patients are in their teens or early twenties, with some cases being detected when the patient is in their thirties. It is important to understand that schizophrenia does not develop later in life, but it simply remains dormant enough to stay undetected. Generally speaking, the earlier the individual is diagnosed, the higher their chances of effectively managing their symptoms and leading a normal life.

Who Is More at Risk of Developing Schizophrenia?

There is a myriad of risk factors associated with schizophrenia. At times, the disorder can appear out of the blue and have no clear cause. However, in other cases, genetics and environmental causes can play a huge role in causing the condition. The general consensus suggests that some individuals are more prone than others to developing this disorder. Here is a breakdown of a few of the common risk factors of schizophrenia:

• **Race:** There is currently no conclusive evidence to suggest that race is in any way connected to this illness. Yet, people of afro origins have recently been shown to be more susceptible to developing schizophrenia. On the other hand, Latino individuals are less at risk. However, more studies need to be done to confirm this.

• **Gender:** Men are more genetically predisposed to schizophrenia. The reason remains unknown, but women are generally more receptive to treatment and experience fewer episodes. This increases their chances of effectively managing their symptoms when compared to their male counterparts.

- **Genetics:** Heredity is one of the main culprits behind this disorder. People who have a schizophrenic parent are around 15% more at risk of developing this mental illness. Similarly, affected siblings can also increase your chances of becoming schizophrenic by 10%, with a higher risk rate for twins.

- **Birth Complications:** Children whose birth is considered difficult or full of complications are expected to suffer from schizophrenia in their teens or early adulthood. Such complications usually include oxygen deprivation and infections, which have a direct effect on the brain. However, this is not a definitive cause of schizophrenia.

- **Drug Abuse:** Drugs are closely linked to schizophrenia. In this regard, hallucinogenic drugs, in particular, can cause a state of psychosis, which may explain why some heavy cannabis users end up developing schizophrenia later in life.

- **Environment:** Strangely enough, people living in cities or generally urban environments have a higher chance of becoming schizophrenic. Some psychiatrists believe that pollutants and genetics act together to induce the symptoms. However, there is not a lot of research in this area.

Symptoms

Not all patients exhibit the same symptoms, and their intensity also varies from one person to another. You will learn more about the warning signs and symptoms of schizophrenia in later chapters. For now, here is a quick summary:

- **Hallucinations (positive symptom):** This is the most common and well-known symptom. Such hallucinations can be auditory, visual, or both. Patients usually report hearing whispers or seeing people who are not really there. In some cases, the patient can interact with these voices or images.

- **Delusions (positive symptom):** Most patients suffer from delusions related either to themselves or others. These delusions can be ones of grandeur or be more linked to one's faith or beliefs. In some other cases, patients may believe that people are plotting against them or may misconstrue normal gestures as signs of aggression.

- **Thoughts and Diction (negative symptom):** Jumbled thoughts are a common sign of schizophrenia. These muddled ideas may end up affecting the patient's speech as well, rendering it completely random or simply incomprehensible.

- **Weakened Motor Functions (negative symptom):** Sometimes, schizophrenic individuals find themselves unable to run errands or complete chores. They may also pace or excessively move around in general for no particular reason.

- **Depression:** The main reason why many patients who have schizophrenia are misdiagnosed with depression at first is that they may appear detached or unwilling to engage in social activities.

The Impact of Schizophrenia

As schizophrenia is considered a serious mental disorder, it can completely change a person's behavior and thought patterns. The patients who have this illness often report the following effects:

- **Physical Impact:** As we've mentioned briefly, schizophrenia affects patients' motor functions, but their physical complications go beyond that. There is an increased chance of developing type 2 diabetes and high blood pressure in schizophrenic individuals. This was previously linked to the use of antipsychotic drugs. Yet, after monitoring patients who do not rely on medications, psychiatrists reached the same findings. Weight gain is also an indirect result of schizophrenia, as this disorder makes people less motivated to be active.

- **Social Impact:** Schizophrenic individuals are less likely to engage in social activities, often preferring to withdraw from crowds. This makes it harder for them to get the support they need and may even lead to suicide in some severe cases. Considering that many patients complain that they are being ostracized due to the negative stigma surrounding schizophrenia, they need to confide in their loved ones. Their support can help mitigate their symptoms and allow them to integrate into society.

- **Educational Impact:** A considerable number of people affected by schizophrenia are teenagers. Prior to their diagnosis, these teens usually show no signs of being different from their peers, neither socially nor academically. However, schizophrenic episodes can take their toll on these individuals, impairing their cognitive skills. Students who suffer from such a disorder often report having trouble focusing in class and retaining information for long. It is also not uncommon for patients to forgo the activities they used to enjoy before being diagnosed. In the long run, this can negatively reflect on their academic performance, given that many schizophrenic students score lower grades than their classmates.

- **Familial Bonds:** Schizophrenia makes individuals detached and less able to sustain deep emotional connections, even with their family members. Of course, if the patient's family does not know that it is simply a symptom of the disorder, they may think that the patient does not care about them. For this reason, psychiatrists often advise families who have schizophrenic members to make themselves emotionally available, without pressuring the patients to reciprocate if they do not feel like it at the time.

- **Work Performance:** It is generally hard for schizophrenic patients to find decent jobs either due to their low grades in high school or lack of vital skills. Furthermore, schizophrenia might make individuals forgo basic hygiene, which can give their employers the wrong impression about them and prompt them to believe that they cannot handle their job responsibilities. Some managers may also simply be prejudiced against schizophrenia and may not employ those who have this condition in the first place. Patients are recommended to seek occupational therapists who can help them develop their skills and land worthwhile work positions.

Cure

There is currently no definitive cure for schizophrenia, and it is unheard of for people to recover from this disorder completely. However, modern treatment plans make the symptoms very manageable, which enables patients to lead healthy lives. As a general rule of thumb, psychiatrists prescribe antipsychotics to reduce the severity of hallucinations and delusions. Talk therapy is also used to help patients process their thoughts and emotions. In severe cases, however, the patient may need to be admitted into the hospital if they pose a danger to themselves or others. This can be the result of severe schizophrenic episodes. Fortunately, most individuals do not need this type of intervention since they are aided by special social workers who help them navigate life and manage their symptoms, in addition to the aid they get from their therapists. There are also some alternative treatment plans that you will learn more about in upcoming chapters.

Prognosis

With proper treatment, the prognosis of schizophrenic patients is usually positive. Roughly 50% of individuals recover to the point that they can manage their condition independently. Around 25% successfully manage some of their symptoms but continue to need support from therapy and loved ones, while only 15% do not notice any improvement. In most cases, the earlier the patient receives treatment, the higher their chance of recovering. Patients who also have an active lifestyle are less likely to suffer some of the disorder's lethal complications like cardiovascular disease. Despite this relatively positive outlook, suicide is still prevalent among schizophrenic individuals. It is estimated that 10% of patients commit suicide. Male patients are also more prone to ending their lives early compared to female patients.

Support groups, regular therapy sessions, and a strong network of friends are needed to help patients recover more easily and reduce the prevalence of suicide.

Psychiatrists claim that after being on medications for six to nine months, most patients notice a big improvement when it comes to positive symptoms like hallucinations and delusions. There is still a lot to be discovered about schizophrenia, but for the vast majority of people, it remains a fairly manageable disorder.

Chapter 2: Signs and Symptoms

We all have various degrees of misconception related to schizophrenia. Fortunately, a lot of these misconceptions can be dispelled by understanding the early signs and symptoms of schizophrenia. Sure, it can be challenging to recognize this unique disorder, but with keen observation, knowledge, and a hint of subtlety, you should be able to detect schizophrenia with a relative degree of accuracy. It should be noted, though, that the symptoms of schizophrenia are similar to other disorders, so recognizing these symptoms in other people doesn't qualify as an official or accurate diagnosis. In fact, only a certified psychiatrist or a psychologist can tell for sure that someone has schizophrenia.

Warning Signs

Individuals with schizophrenia will typically start exhibiting symptoms around puberty. As mentioned in the previous chapter, most of these individuals are diagnosed in their late teenage years to their early 30s. However, men will more often showcase their symptoms earlier than females (usually in their early to late 20s). Women, on the other hand, are most often diagnosed in their late 20s and early 30s. Early warning signs include withdrawal, isolation, expressionlessness, abandonment, little concern for personal hygiene, insomnia or excessive sleeping, inability to cry or express joy, or conversely, excessive crying. This can also be accompanied by depression. These are typically general symptoms and could apply to other disorders as well. For that reason, we should not jump to conclusions and falsely think that someone is schizophrenic for excessively crying, for example.

• **Adolescence**

There isn't much explanation as to why schizophrenia develops during adolescence, much less why it develops earlier in men than in women. There are only theories entertaining the facts that we already know. One theory suggests that an environmental element activates a certain sequence of genes that a person possesses, which then triggers the symptoms to show. Our brains undergo a lot of changes during puberty, so it wouldn't be too surprising if these changes also activated schizophrenic genes. When it comes to schizophrenia manifesting earlier in men than women, some people theorize that estrogen somehow delays these symptoms.

- **The Early-Onset and Late-Onset**

Early-onset schizophrenia affects some children younger than 13 years old, causing a host of schizophrenic warning signs like late talking, late crawling or walking, withdrawal, depression, unusual movements, irregular sleeping patterns, and alcohol or drug abuse. Late-onset schizophrenia, which is diagnosed after the age of 45, is suspected to be due to the supposedly schizophrenic genes being activated at a late stage of a person's life. People with late-onset schizophrenia may not exhibit negative symptoms, but they will be affected by all the usual symptoms of schizophrenia-like delusions, hallucinations, and trouble understanding information.

- **Prevalence of Schizophrenia**

Schizophrenia affects as many as 20 million people around the world, with 3.5 million schizophrenic people in the U.S. alone. Despite these large numbers, schizophrenia is not as common as other mental disorders like anxiety disorders or eating disorders. However, symptoms of these mental illnesses can be quite similar in nature, and they can be easily confused. For that reason, getting an expert's diagnosis is the first step a person can take toward effectively treating their symptoms. Of course, mild cases of schizophrenia are not as distinct as more serious cases, where individuals will exhibit violent symptoms like emotional disturbances and psychosis.

Symptoms

Symptoms of schizophrenia usually revolve around cognitive abilities. People with schizophrenia often don't have full command over their cognitive faculties. That's why they will often experience hallucinations, delusions, and disorganized thinking. However, one should note that not all symptoms will appear at the same time, as a lot of people will be affected by other symptoms at a later stage of their life. Some people, on the other hand, are able to recover from some symptoms thanks to effective treatments, but other symptoms, unfortunately, are always present. The severity of these symptoms can change depending on the age of the patient and the type of treatment they are receiving.

- **Delusions**

As you likely know, delusions are false beliefs that a person firmly holds on to, even if there's no supporting evidence to their plausibility. This is probably the most common symptom schizophrenic people have (about 90% of people with schizophrenia experience delusions in various degrees of severity). Knowing whether or not someone is delusional is easy, as their strong thoughts and beliefs will sound outlandish to other people. Thinking that a gesture is meant to cause you harm, or always thinking that something bad is about to happen could be considered as delusional thought, especially when it has no evidence to back it up. Here are some broader examples of delusions:

1. Control

Delusions of control, or lack thereof, are thoughts that an individual has when they think that an external force is taking control over their life in every way possible. If someone thinks that someone is listening to their every thought and broadcasting them, even though it is an inconceivable thing to think, then they have delusions of control. Similarly, if someone is thinking that there is an alien force implanting or removing thoughts from their head, they are definitely having delusions of control.

2. Reference

This is a type of delusion where a person believes that certain events they experience, or witness, are solely directed at them. They might see a message in every object that they see in their environment. They may notice non-existing patterns in irrelevant information, so you can see how these delusions can constantly plague someone's thought patterns. If a patient has delusions of reference, for example, they may think that a song that was playing on the radio was meant for them or that news that they have read in a bulletin is targeting them. This type of delusion places its victims under a state of paranoia at all times.

3. Persecution

Constant thoughts of believing that everyone means you harm exemplifies delusions of persecution. This type of delusion involves being paranoid and scared of people trying to harm the person in question with bizarre methods, such as a rare poisonous formula, for example. If someone has delusions of persecution, they will often fear being in ordinary situations, i.e. fearing that their food may be poisoned. They may be extremely distressed all the time, report un-real events to authorities, and be constantly seeking help and attention regarding their safety and well-being.

4. Grandeur

Delusions of grandeur, or grandiose delusions, refer to false beliefs that the person in question is an important figure, which often leads a person to regard themselves from a megalomaniac perspective. A person with delusions of grandeur is not above thinking that they are a supernatural entity, possessing telekinetic, pyrokinetic, or hydrokinetic powers. Not all people with these delusions are necessarily schizophrenic, but these are one of the most common delusions a schizophrenic person could possess. Like all other types of delusions, a person doesn't need any facts or evidence to disprove their delusions, as these beliefs are deeply instilled in their minds.

• **Hallucinations**

As you may already know, hallucinations are sounds, sensations, and visions that only one person experiences. Because these hallucinations involve all of their senses, a schizophrenic person will have a hard time telling the truth from reality when experiencing them. These hallucinations often make sense to the ones experiencing them, so if they are hearing someone talking to them, that voice may sound familiar, despite how aggressive or vulgar their tone is. Auditory hallucinations are usually the most common type that schizophrenic people experience, but visual hallucinations are also not uncommon. In any case, having hallucinations when they're alone can be the worst thing that could happen to a schizophrenic individual, as they won't be able to discern truth from reality.

- **Thought Disorder**

This disorder is probably the main cause of disorganized speech. Because of the individual's inability to organize their thoughts, they will have trouble formulating coherent sentences. Thus, people may have a difficult time understanding what they're trying to say. They might, as a result, stop talking in the middle of a sentence because the thought that inspired them to speak has suddenly disappeared. People with thought disorders will also give non-sequiturs to questions directed at them, confusing their conversation partners even more. Their speech will include what's known as 'word salad,' which is a formation or a combination of unrelated words that don't make sense as a unit. These signs can be clear enough for anyone conversing with a person who has thought disorder, but there are other signs with which you can recognize disorganized speech:

1. **Neologism**

Neologism is the invention of new words or phrases, which, in the case of a schizophrenic person, only makes sense to their inventor. While this skill is impressive in its own right, using neologism excessively in speech will add an unnecessary layer of ambiguity, which will make a conversation unproductive instantly, unless of course, these made-up words are explained in detail for the sake of entertainment or for furthering the conversation.

2. Repetition

Schizophrenic people with strong disorganized speech will repeat sentences and words that they like to the point that they don't make sense anymore. In fact, they may use them even when they don't fit in the context. This tendency to repeat things over and over is a testament to how scrambled their thoughts are.

3. Clang

Clang, or the use of rhyming words, is another characteristic of disorganized speech. The witty usage of rhyming words can often add a light tone to a conversation, but only when it goes along with the context of a conversation. If it doesn't, which is usually the case for a schizophrenic person, they would otherwise be meaningless and wouldn't add much to the value of the conversation.

4. Unconnected Thoughts

As mentioned above, people with thought disorders have an unorganized mind. Their thoughts are always in clutter, and they, more often than not, lose track of what they were thinking about. This will make their sentences chopped, and their speech disconnected without a single connection that makes sense. They will jump from one topic to another in the hopes that the other person will comprehend what they're getting at.

• Disorganized Behavior

In a similar nature to the way thoughts are disorganized and disconnected, schizophrenic patients will find themselves at a disadvantage when directing their motor abilities. They also won't be able to carry out the simple tasks of initiating and holding a conversation, taking care of their health and well-being, and doing their work. You can notice this in a person's behavior if they show unpredictable emotional responses, childlike behavior, strange behavior such as adopting a bizarre posture, impulsive actions, and excessive movement.

• Negative Symptoms

Negative symptoms are the lack of normal behaviors in otherwise fully-functioning individuals. This can lead to reduced functionality in patients of schizophrenia. Their relationships will usually weaken over time and diminish entirely. Negative symptoms include an inability to self-express, lack of interest in the world, reduced enthusiasm, and interests similar to the ones found in depressed patients, as well as speech difficulties. While previous symptoms might not always be present, especially in social activities, negative symptoms alone can alienate schizophrenic patients from society and even segregate them, which can lead to inconsolable damage to their psyche.

- **Psychosis**

The worst symptom that schizophrenic patients experience is episodes of psychosis. Doctors refer to schizophrenia as a type of psychosis, so this symptom is most common. However, the frequency of these episodes, along with their severity, will typically change depending on the person experiencing them. For example, some people may only experience one psychotic episode in the span of their lives, while others may experience them more consistently but still lead a normal life in the intermittent time between those episodes. A full-fledged psychotic episode will reveal significant and bizarre changes in behavior, leading to emotional confusion, breakdowns, and a sense of anxiety.

Now that you know the symptoms of schizophrenia, you should have a greater understanding of what a loved one with schizophrenia is experiencing. Though there are no definitive treatments for schizophrenia, there are many options for managing its symptoms, which will be explored in future chapters. These will help schizophrenic patients retain and maintain control over their lives.

Chapter 3: How to Diagnose Schizophrenia

Schizophrenia is a very difficult disorder to manage and understand. Its antecedents and diagnosis have evolved throughout the years, but researchers continue to work hard to try and untangle this singular mental illness and figure out what causes it. For the most part, it may very well be genetic, yet studies continue to dissect its history and understand how to diagnose it better.

This disorder is known to debilitate an individual's ability to form clear thoughts, handle emotions, or even relate to others. It is a deeply complex condition and is usually properly diagnosed when a person is in their twenties or thirties. If it is correctly diagnosed early on, it is absolutely possible to lead a normal life with the condition. The following are some ways in which it is possible to diagnose schizophrenia.

Schizophrenia in Young Individuals

The younger the patient is, the more difficult it can be to diagnose the condition accurately. It is not immediately evident in many individuals what the symptoms will look like in a teenager, since the behavioral patterns are rather nonspecific. For example, the first warning signs can be a drop in academic performance, irritability, a change in social dynamics, and a questionable group of friends - all of which can occur with teenagers regardless of their mental health issues.

However, other behavioral patterns can raise some red flags more readily. For example, the teenager may begin to isolate themselves and withdraw from those around them. They may vocalize unusual ideas or suspicions that do not align with our common understanding of today's current social climate. This may be the first piece of evidence of turmoil rearing its ugly head. The young individual's brain is still developing in this stage, so most doctors would be hesitant to make a diagnosis early on, but they will likely continue to monitor the individual's development in case the matter becomes clearer over the following years. This stage is typically referred to as the 'prodromal period.'

Symptoms

Eventually, a comprehensive medical examination will be ordered so that the best and most accurate diagnosis can be ascertained. A few key symptoms should be evident for at least six months so that professionals can properly assess whether or not the patient has schizophrenia. The complete breakdown of symptoms are as follows:

• **Hallucinations**

This is a common telltale sign. If the individual in question reports seeing, hearing, or even smelling things that others cannot perceive, this is a sign of hallucinations at work. These experiences feel very real to them, so the only people privy to this distortion of reality could be loved ones, acquaintances, teachers, or anyone else in their immediate vicinity who can vouch for the occurrence. Hallucinations can have roots in the immediate reality around them; say, they can imagine a confidant to be speaking to them. Alternatively, these hallucinations can be complete fabrications that the patient has created and imagined entirely on their own.

• **Lack of Emotion**

An inability to feel or show empathy, or to even express their emotions positively is another telltale sign. This is also called a negative symptom, and it often entails a person speaking in dull, flat tones, with a distinct inability to express themselves fully. Individuals may also show little interest in activities, sustaining relationships, and so on. This symptom, while a red herring for a schizophrenia diagnosis, is also commonly confused with clinical depression. For this reason, clinicians tread carefully around this symptom and try to find more signs of the illness other than negative symptoms alone.

• Cognitive Issues

Limited cognitive capacity, or scattered thinking, is another major symptom of schizophrenia. This means that sufferers may have trouble remembering things, keeping their thoughts organized, and generally face difficulty in completing tasks. This aspect of the disease can be rather challenging since the individual will often have trouble realizing that they are struggling with this symptom, and it would mean getting someone from their immediate circle to vouch for the fact that it is an issue.

• Delusional Thinking

This is different from hallucinating since it refers to actual beliefs held by the patient that are patently false; it's not a matter of them imagining things off and on in a kind of fugue state. These delusional thoughts do not change even when the patient is being presented with a different set of facts about events and people around them. The individual in question may also have trouble concentrating, may be prone to confused thinking, and have their thought processes feel blocked, or hindered.

• Becoming Catatonic

A frequent marker of a schizophrenic patient is the sudden fall into a catatonic state, staring off into the distance at nothing in particular, in a complete daze. The patient may not even speak or verbalize their thoughts for some time. They may be lost in a world of their own, and they typically do not remember this when they emerge from this state.

• Hyperactive Behavior

In addition to falling into a catatonic state, the patient may revert to another extreme in the form of bouts of hyperactivity. This sudden spurt of energy will seem manic, bizarre, and not coherent in relation to anything else that they may have tried to express earlier. It will, of course, feel completely disjointed from any catatonic state they may have fallen into previously.

How to Get a Correct Diagnosis

The first step to having schizophrenia correctly diagnosed is by seeing a licensed and experienced physician or psychiatrist. Only a licensed medical professional can help you get an accurate diagnosis of this complex condition. The doctor will order a full psychological evaluation alongside a medical exam. They will also request a complete medical history from the family and find out if there are other mental health issues in the family tree. They will also require statements from people in the patient's circle regarding the individual's behavior in the past to establish any apparent changes in their demeanor and mental faculties. This full examination and notation of the patient's medical history will occur regardless of whether or not they have been recently hospitalized. These details are incredibly important and crucial to forming a thorough understanding of the patient's history.

In addition, there are a few other, seemingly aberrant tests that the physician or psychiatrist may request. For one, urine and blood tests may be needed in order to ensure that some of the symptoms listed above are not the result of alcohol or drug abuse - hard drugs, in particular, can cause severe hallucinations and dissociation from reality.

By the same token, an MRI and CT scan of the body and brain will likely be requested to cross off the possibility of a brain tumor. There will also be several cognitive and personality tests taken to accurately measure the extent to which an individual understands cues and can glean meaning from information presented to them, while inkblot tests can attest to the ways in which the patient views the world.

To wrap up the findings from the diagnostic tests, the psychiatric evaluation will be completed by the mental health professional. They will observe and fully account for the patient's appearance and demeanor, while going over a few questions regarding moods, delusions, substance abuse, and any suicidal ideations. The doctor will then refer to the Diagnostic and Statistical Manual of Mental Disorders (commonly known as the DSM-5) to complete the assessment. Combined, these tests help to establish a clearer picture of where the patient is in their journey, and this can allow medical professionals to put together a holistic plan to help manage the disorder.

Treatment Plans

Obtaining an early diagnosis can help improve the patient's chances of being able to conquer and effectively manage the illness. Proper care and a good treatment plan will include a combination of medication, psychotherapy, and talk therapy. Schizophrenia mandates lifelong treatment and follow-ups to manage the condition, and sometimes, a longer hospital stay may be required. A full team approach is usually taken to help treat the disorder, and there will typically be more than one professional tasked with helping the patient to manage the symptoms and keep them at bay.

A thorough set of medications is the basis for the treatment of schizophrenia, especially antipsychotics, since they are thought to control symptoms by affecting the brain's neurotransmitters and its capacity to produce dopamine. The ultimate goal of the treatment is to manage signs and symptoms at the lowest possible dose. The patient may need to try different kinds of drugs at first, or at least different doses and combinations over a duration of time to achieve the equilibrium that might best help them to achieve the required results. In addition to the antipsychotics, antidepressants and anti-anxiety medications may also be assigned to help treat the illness, and it will typically take a few weeks or even months to see improvement in the condition.

Unfortunately, the medication for schizophrenia can engender difficult side effects, and it may be difficult to convince the patient to remain on the course for a long period of time.

Immediate medical treatment usually alleviates any psychosis induced symptoms, and this will be the main focus. However, long term treatment evolves to encompass the medication, as well as any psychological and social assistance that the medical professional sees fit. These include but are not limited to individual therapy, social training, or "re-entry" programs into society, familial therapy, and so on.

The psychotherapy part of the treatment can gradually assist in normalizing the patient's thought patterns, which also teaches them to cope with stress and understand some of the warning signs of relapse so that they can avoid major episodes.

In terms of training for social skills, these sessions are meant to help improve the patient's communication skills and capabilities to function in social situations once more. This can ensure that working and everyday tasks can once again be performed in a manner that feels natural, and that will not bring about any episodes of psychosis or anxiety.

The treatment plans should also be formulated in a way that helps enrich the patient's social circle. For example, family therapy is set up to provide support and help educate family members who have to learn new coping skills in order to deal with the schizophrenic loved one. That said, medical professionals can help with the patient's professional goals by getting them rehabilitated vocationally and finding supported employment. In this way, they can help people with schizophrenia find jobs they like, and also learn how to keep those jobs despite the condition.

Schizophrenia is, again, a complicated disorder, and one whose diagnosis can be rather difficult. Diagnosis can be just as difficult as creating an action plan that provides adequate support for the patient. Getting treatment to nip any potential psychotic episode in the bud is crucial. Most individuals with schizophrenia also require a good network to provide daily support to help them manage the illness. Community-based programs that offer job support help with housing, offer talk-therapy groups, and crisis management networks are all crucial for the individual's long-term health and self-esteem. Sometimes, a social worker will be the one to help assign the patient to different resources that can help them move forward with living a healthy and well-rounded life.

Pop culture arguably stigmatizes schizophrenia more than other mental illnesses. There are a lot of clichés out there, and it can be hard to tell the difference between the representations sanctioned by this moving image versus reality, which is harder and less glamorous. However, the good news is if schizophrenia is diagnosed early on, it can be properly managed, and the patient can go on to lead a full and happy life. The key is early diagnosis and the creation of a social network that can help support the patient through difficult times.

Chapter 4: Treatment

Schizophrenia does not have a cure; however, different treatments can help schizophrenic patients deal with the varying symptoms that they are facing and aid them as well as their families in managing the illness. There are different types of treatments that can be combined together, or used separately, to reach the optimal treatment for patients individually. The treatment used for schizophrenia depends largely on the severity of the case, and the intensity of the episodes one might face.

Length of Schizophrenia Treatments

As mentioned above, schizophrenia treatments are only used to limit symptoms and to make this disorder more manageable, not to cure the patient completely. This is why the treatment for schizophrenia does not stop after a couple of months or even years. It is something that people with schizophrenia have to receive in different dosages and plans for their entire lives. Over time, of course, the treatment is adjusted to fit the requirements of the person suffering from this illness. A very encouraging fact is that after approximately five years of receiving treatment, a significant improvement is typically seen, especially if the illness was diagnosed early on.

Who is Responsible for Giving and Following Up on Treatments?

If you or a loved one is concerned about how they will receive their treatment and who will be responsible for following up, rest assured that there will be a specific team responsible for giving the person the proper care and continuous support to stop the disorder from progressing. The person can usually resume their life with some semblance of normalcy. The name of the team that is responsible for providing such care is usually known as the Community Mental Health Team. It will comprise of social workers and a variety of healthcare personnel, including specialized certified nurses, pharmacists, and psychiatrists. These people are dedicated to helping different patients deal with schizophrenia, while simultaneously allowing their patients to exercise their independence. A whole team takes on this job because, as mentioned above, more than one treatment is usually given to a person with schizophrenia.

Antipsychotic Medication

Most schizophrenia treatments include medication. There are two main types of medication that a schizophrenic individual can take to help him or her with their symptoms. They are split into typical and atypical antipsychotic medications. The difference between these two types of antipsychotic medication was actually the years when they were developed. The first type, Typicals, includes antipsychotics that were developed before the 1950s, while the second type, Atypicals, includes medication that was developed afterward, specifically in the 1990s. Antipsychotic Medication is often used initially to reduce the effect of dopamine on the brain, thus decreasing the aggression and anxiety levels experienced by schizophrenic patients. To have any kind of effect on long term symptoms such as hallucinations, however, a person needs to take such medications for a week or more.

Before a patient starts taking antipsychotic meds, they need to be fully aware of the benefits and the various side-effects that they can incur while they are on them. Usually, the patient is informed about these side-effects by their psychiatrist. Side-effects that can commonly be caused by typical antipsychotic medications include shaking and muscle spasms. On the other hand, the common side-effects of atypical antipsychotics include drowsiness and blurred vision.

Cognitive Behaviour Therapy

This type of therapy focuses on a person's behavior rather than other factors that affect schizophrenia. When a schizophrenia-diagnosed person is treated by CBT or Cognitive Behaviour Therapy, they are taught to consciously alter their way of thinking and behavior so that they are able to deal with schizophrenic symptoms such as hallucinations, delusions, and episode triggers before they become dangerous. Usually, CBT is accompanied by medication that will work to lessen the symptoms themselves. There are quite a few benefits of CBT, including raising self-esteem, creating positive thoughts, and improving coping methods and skills, to name a few. All of these benefits provided by Cognitive Behaviour Therapy create a strong foundation of support for the person undertaking it. This foundation, in turn, enables them to handle the disorder much more effectively. Just like any other type of therapy, CBT requires constant follow up and communication between the patient and their therapists.

Family Therapy

As the name of this treatment suggests, family therapy mainly centers on how a patient's family can contribute to the treatment of a schizophrenic individual. A large part of a person's treatment is the kind of support that they receive from the people they trust. This disorder has a lot of negative stigmas associated with it, as well as exaggerations, because people seldom educate themselves thoroughly on the matter. This can lead to families being unable to show proper support for their loved ones because they do not always know what to do. Family therapy helps open more efficient communication pathways between the patients in question and their families and friends. This not only ensures that family members are fully aware of what their loved one needs, but they can also learn ways to help them cope with different symptoms.

Arts Therapy

This is an expressive, rather than just a communicative, type of therapy. Arts therapy helps schizophrenic individuals to center themselves and to express their thoughts, fears, worries, and general feelings into various forms of art. This form of therapy is very subjective and is tailored based on the person's preferred form of expression. Different types of art therapy that have been incorporated in schizophrenia treatments include painting, writing poems, short stories, coloring, singing, and various forms of dance. Although it seems insignificant or irrelevant to schizophrenia, it has been proven through different studies that art therapy has a positive effect on patients trying to cope with schizophrenia. This type of treatment also helps patients by allowing them different ways to express what they want to communicate, helping them concentrate, and, most importantly, reducing the level of isolation that they feel because of their diagnosis. Arts therapy also plays a role in increasing a person's level of self-awareness, which is necessary for a person dealing with schizophrenia so that they can detect their triggers and the different signs that their bodies and brains give them before an episode.

Individual Psychotherapy

Individual psychotherapy focuses more on helping the person understand themselves and becoming even more self-aware, and it is a form of treatment that the patient receives from a psychiatrist rather than a therapist. This type of psychotherapy urges and aids schizophrenics to normalize their thought patterns as much as possible. However, most significantly, individual psychotherapy can help patients detect when they are going to have a relapse by recognizing early warning signs. As such, they can take proactive measures to ensure that they and everyone around them are safe. Individual psychotherapy is more focused on one person, and sessions do not include anyone other than the patient and their psychiatrist.

Cognitive Enhancement Therapy

Cognitive Enhancement Therapy or CET is a type of therapy that is considered by many as helpful for people diagnosed with schizophrenia. This is because of the reasoning that this illness is a brain disorder affecting different functions such as attention and memory. These affected areas are very likely to remain seriously hindered even after the person receiving treatment takes medication to limit other more obvious symptoms such as hallucinations. CET gives schizophrenic people a way to regain their short, and long-term memory, as well as retain their attention span through a variety of mentally beneficial exercises they can practice with their therapist or on their own. Another name for this type of therapy is cognitive remediation. Benefits of Cognitive Enhancement Therapy include a raised level of self-awareness, better recognition of social cues or triggers, and an improved ability to organize their thoughts in a coherent manner.

Electroconvulsive Therapy

This therapy is clouded by a wide range of stigma and misinformation that tarnishes its reputation as an effective type of therapy. Some people believe that electroconvulsive therapy is a form of barbaric torture. However, various studies have proven that in some cases, electroconvulsive therapy is one of the most successful methods to help patients manage schizophrenia, especially after severe episodes or relapses. It is also used to treat severe depression. What many people do not realize is that professionals use a device that merely stimulates the brain by sending little electric currents to the brain, while the person receiving the treatment is under anesthesia. This type of therapy was formerly known as electroshock therapy. Before the therapy is administered, a psychiatrist speaks with their schizophrenic patient extensively about their rights. They will also explain what to expect before, during, and after the procedure. This type of therapy is not one that is used right away when a person is diagnosed with schizophrenia, however, because it is most effective for those who suffer from the later stages of schizophrenia.

Hospitalization

When schizophrenic people hear the word hospitalization, they often immediately associate it with being forcefully detained. However, there are actually two kinds of hospitalization. The first kind is when a patient admits themselves to a hospital or care center that specializes in treating schizophrenia so that they can receive their treatment without any setbacks. Then they can leave once they believe that they can handle their illness. Of course, in that case, the person still has to keep in contact with a specialized team so that they can track their progress and find out if they need any sort of ongoing help. The other kind of hospitalization can be considered a detainment, but it is not very common. This detainment only occurs when a person's doctor has serious concerns regarding their patient's safety or the safety of those around them. Only then would the option of compulsory hospitalization be considered.

If a person is hospitalized, they do not necessarily have to spend the rest of their lives inside. They can go back to their normal lives after receiving the treatments that they need to limit the symptoms that have resulted in them being hospitalized in the first place.

Self-Help Measures

Treatment is not limited to what a professional can provide. A person diagnosed with schizophrenia can take certain measures to help speed up their treatment and to ensure that they do not have a relapse in the future. The first thing that one can do is surround themselves with a strong support system. This can be in the form of friends, family, or even support groups for people going through the same experiences that they are facing. The second is to relieve themselves of stress as much as possible. Stress negatively affects a person's mental health, and when it comes to someone who is already trying to deal with an illness, it can have an even worse effect. A person who has schizophrenia can also adjust their diet to include healthier foods and become more active to ensure that anxiety and depression are better controlled.

Factors that Aid Treatment

Different factors can affect the length of time one needs to get back on their feet and resume their lives normally when managing their schizophrenia. As mentioned above, one of these factors is having the support of others, which is why family therapy and surrounding oneself with supportive people is very important. Other factors include how early the diagnosis is made, and whether there is regular follow up with the specialized team or not.

These different treatments are quite effective and have helped many people with schizophrenia over the years. While getting treated for schizophrenia is ongoing, and currently there is no cure, with the right care, attitude, and help, one can expect to live a fulfilling and happy life. When looking for different treatment options, it is important to consult a doctor and communicate openly with others so that the best course of action can be determined.

Chapter 5: How to Manage Schizophrenia

What makes schizophrenia so complex is that it's not an illness that can easily be diagnosed. A person with schizophrenia can go from having episodes of psychosis to showcasing complete mental stability during a short period of time. While it's not curable, it is definitely manageable, but dealing with schizophrenia is, unfortunately, an ongoing process. There is currently no cure for it or any treatment that will eliminate the symptoms forever. However, the combination of medication, supportive therapies, and self-help strategies can help reduce the symptoms and assist in learning how to control their severity. Most people who suffer from this illness learn how to control it within a maximum of five years of being diagnosed. However, one may still face challenges after this time. Managing symptoms and controlling the frequency and recurrence of those episodes are processes that can be learned over time. In this chapter, we will discuss what it means to oversee and manage these symptoms, how to get the support you or a loved one needs, and how to create a life that is suitable for the patient.

Controlling Mindsets

People who have been diagnosed with schizophrenia may experience great levels of distress. They may also experience a tremendous decrease in their self-esteem and confidence, as well as an understanding that their diagnosis is a life-changing event. However, diagnosis is a tool that helps schizophrenics with their journey of recovery; accepting the condition is the first step in the recovery process. Following up with a mental health professional, taking prescribed medications, making sure that the right people surround the patient, and knowing that they can talk to them beyond their condition to express how they feel are all keys to speeding up their recovery. The patient needs to be honest with their doctors and mental health professionals about what they experience from their perspective, and also notify their physicians of side effects from their medications. If the dose or the medicine doesn't work for the patient for any reason, they should be able to talk to their doctor about changing the dosage or switching to another medication.

Being schizophrenic doesn't mean the patient in question can't live a healthy life. For that reason, they have to make sure that they set milestones, goals, and plans for their life. The best way to deal with schizophrenia is to stay busy with work, hobbies, and interests as well as staying away from stress by meditating and practicing mindfulness. Patients need to also surround themselves with those who make them feel the most comfortable, and safe.

Finding the Right Treatment

As mentioned above, managing schizophrenia revolves around finding the right combination of medications, following self-help plans, and surrounding the patient with the right people. If an individual has been experiencing symptoms indicative of schizophrenia and has talked to a mental health professional before these signs worsen, their chances of managing the disorder are high. Although patients can't solely depend on medications that mental health professionals suggest, it's essential for the patient and their loved ones to fully understand the medication's side effects. The patient should be aware of their rights to request a replacement if they can't handle the side effects of a particular drug.

Patients also should educate themselves about schizophrenia and make sure to build a reliable support system through group sessions and family therapy. That said, lifestyle changes are never a complete solution to a mental illness that is as confusing and multifaceted as schizophrenia. Still, a few changes in lifestyle can have a large impact. Experiment with making changes to your diet, communication, exercise, and work patterns, and you will likely notice an improvement in the way you feel. Self-care and medication can combine well to decrease the chances of a person having a schizophrenic episode, and also lower the severity of their symptoms. You need to keep in mind that the more you try to maintain a positive attitude, the easier it will be to relieve the symptoms.

Keep in mind that treatment for Schizophrenia is usually customized to each person's specific needs. The patient needs to make sure that they have a say in the treatment process. Their concerns and preferences must be taken into consideration. Treatment is most efficient when it's combined with lifestyle changes, medication, and being surrounded by those who love and support the patient the most.

Create a Supportive Environment

Communication and human interaction are vital for a person who's suffering from Schizophrenia. During episodes of Schizophrenia, a person might tend to become more isolated, paranoid, and filled with anger. Staying in touch with family, friends, and loved ones that can listen and provide support can be extremely helpful. Talking to someone who provides love and support can help a Schizophrenic become more functional. There are plenty of support groups for those who have Schizophrenia where they can talk and share their feelings with those who can understand them the most.

If you're reading this because someone you know has been recently diagnosed with Schizophrenia, then you should understand a few things. Talking to a Schizophrenic about how they feel can be hard, but one needs to be persistent and have patience. Therefore, one must try to break the ice and give them the freedom to express their deepest and darkest thoughts without judging or taking actions that might make them feel uncomfortable.

Develop a Healthy Routine

Since there isn't a specific treatment method for Schizophrenia, you shouldn't rely on medication and alone to get better. A patient can also make a few changes to their lifestyle that will help them to better manage their symptoms. It is recommended to develop a daily routine that includes exercise, healthy meals, and meditation. If they can take care of themselves in these areas, it will give them a sense of control over their life, as well as their emotional and mental well-being.

Being able to work is also very beneficial, as it allows a person to feel like they're part of something bigger than themselves. Being able to achieve something every day can provide considerable comfort to those who have Schizophrenia.

Avoid Drugs

Many individuals that have Schizophrenia tend to turn to drug abuse. Most of the time, it's because they experience high levels of stress and anxiety and don't know how to deal with it. In that case, getaway drugs and substances can seem like the perfect solution, when really, it just makes things worse. Drugs and substance abuse will only complicate Schizophrenia and can make episodes worse. It can also affect sleep patterns, which are crucial for recovery and overall wellbeing.

Seek Different Kinds of Therapy

It is recommended to try different types of therapy to help manage symptoms, as different therapy types will all approach the symptoms in different ways. For example, art therapy is a common practice in mental health institutions around the world. It allows the patient to express their emotions creatively, which can lead to reestablishing their identity. Drawing can also help them understand their feelings and provide creative solutions as to how they can deal with them. Music therapy can also be helpful.

Try to Understand Themselves Better

It's important for a person to know what causes them to have a schizophrenic episode. It's common for people with Schizophrenia to be triggered by social gatherings and crowded places, though each person's triggers will be unique to them. It's wise to take notes about what things occurred prior to previous episodes so that you can narrow down what might have caused the schizophrenic behavior to manifest in the first place.

Chapter 6: How to Help a Loved One with Schizophrenia

Understanding and empathizing with the fact that a patient's illness is something shocking to them, and that is as frightening and alienating to them as it is to you, is a smart place to start when helping someone diagnosed with Schizophrenia. Whether your loved one is receiving treatment or whether you are reluctant to show them the respect that they deserve for handling an illness that is fraught with difficulties, this chapter will familiarize you with how you can approach the subject with a loved one, and how you can provide them with the support that they need during and after treatment.

Accepting It

Around 3.2 million Americans have this disorder. It most commonly occurs or becomes noticeable during the teenage years, and then reaches a peak of vulnerability between ages 16 and 25. Once schizophrenia occurs, symptoms are recurrent, and they persist with different degrees of severity for the rest of a person's lifetime. It might sound like a life-sentence, and in a way, it is because there is no cure for it. However, when help is offered at the early stages, a patient can be completely functional, hold down a job, get married, have a family, and enjoy their life the way they want to.

Knowing this should make the journey less stressful. You need to learn to accept your loved one the way they are and have reasonable expectations of them. There will be difficulties and days when they will not be able to do anything, and days when they are moody, depressed, and unable to focus. However, there will also be good days when they can achieve a lot.

When accommodating a loved one, make sure to avoid doing the things that they can do for themselves. The idea is to empower the person, rather than infantilize them or spoon-feed them. Good days come at times when there is minimal or no stress on the person. Stress can flare up an episode, so you want to keep your loved one away from stress as much as possible.

That said, communication is key, so talk openly about the illness with them when they are up for it. If you need clarification about the treatment or diagnosis, it is alright to ask the person and let them explain. This is common when dealing with any sort of mental illness. However, some people may just want to sweep it under the rug, but that is never the route to take.

Educate Yourself

The best way to help someone diagnosed with schizophrenia is to help yourself first by learning and understanding as much as you can about this disorder. You can do this in different ways.

There is no lack of information on the internet that can help guide and teach you. Alternatively, you can take a trip to your local library for extensive research on the matter. Obviously, this book is a fantastic place to start! Because schizophrenia has a broad scope, living with a schizophrenic patient or dealing with the person daily can create many different outcomes. Whether or not the person is in question consistently experiences manic episodes, the first thing you will learn is that the illness does not define who the person is. You want to view the person as who they are and avoid letting the diagnosis change your perception of them. Schizophrenic people have their good days and bad days, just like your average person.

Besides reading about it, consider joining a support group or an online community. Support groups aren't a suggestion more than they are a necessity. Joining a group makes you feel less isolated, reduces stress and anxiety, and it fills the gap between medical treatments and emotional instability.

Some groups are led by professionals and official organizations, while others may be run by laypeople who are going through the same thing as you. Both types of groups may sometimes bring in professional experts to talk to the group.

You also have the choice of face-to-face meetings or online conferencing. The most common places to find a support group would be from a recommendation by a doctor, clinic, hospital, or non-profit organizations that lobby for specific medical problems. You can also browse websites of national health institutes. Before joining a group, there are a few things you should ask first. These include:

- How is the group organized and led?

- Is it free?

- How often and how long are the meetings, and where are they held?

- Are meetings ongoing or for a specific time period?

- What happens in a typical meeting?

- How is confidentiality managed?

It is natural to be apprehensive about joining a group and sharing your personal experience with a bunch of people that you don't know. However, there is no pressure on you to talk, and you can learn a lot just by listening. After a couple of meetings, if you start to feel comfortable, you might choose to open up, and even start befriending others in the same situation as yourself.

The reason why support groups are being emphasized is that they are a way of taking care of yourself while getting educated at the same time. It is also a way of building a network of people who can support one another.

Psycho-Education

One of the ways create better communication within the family is to attend psycho-education classes. Sometimes, these are offered by support groups. Family members need to accommodate the person in question and never act as if a burden is placed upon them. You need to be patient and avoid arguing, belittling, or questioning a request of theirs.

The way feelings are communicated within a family contributes to the impact of this condition. Psycho-education has evolved after being established around three decades ago. It has been found that families with a lot of negative experiences, aggressive remarks, and other adverse encounters with those diagnosed with schizophrenia had a much worse outcome than families who dealt with schizophrenia in a more understanding fashion.

As part of the therapy, the condition is discussed with the family to help them understand the illness and introduce them to alternative ways of coping.

Encourage Them to Seek Help and Continue Treatment

We often think that as long as someone is not hurting themselves or others, then we shouldn't advocate that they find treatment. For the most part, this is true. Most schizophrenic individuals are not dangerous, and they are also not monsters nor criminals, but that doesn't mean that treatment is not needed.

Around 70% to 80% of schizophrenics hear voices and sounds at some point. It may or may not reach a point of danger, as sometimes they may only hear their name called, while at other times, it is an argumentative voice that they communicate with. The voice can get louder and more persuasive over time. In serious cases, it can be a threatening voice and one that orders a person to do something.

These voices can be continuous, annoying, and so distracting to the point that the patient decides to follow the voice's orders. Voices that encourage self-harm or harm inflicted on others have to be approached very carefully by a professional.

No medical condition should reach a dangerous level before help is received. You cannot force a person to seek help, but you can listen to their concerns about treatment and what they presume about it.

For a start, know that your loved one wants to communicate; they just don't want to be judged, stigmatized, told what to do, have their freedom constrained, have responsibility and trust taken away from them, or deprived of having a say in their treatment.

If you are having problems convincing a loved one to receive help, you could try to focus on one aspect of the illness. For instance, you will probably see your child, spouse, or whoever the person in question is having episodes of withdrawal, showing lack of interest in others or social activities, or experiencing insomnia or a general lack of energy. You can suggest a visit to the doctor to deal with that specific symptom. You need to acknowledge that the person in question is facing fears of being labeled "crazy," which is one of the main things that may scare them from seeking treatment.

Always try to provide options. The patient may be a loved one, but you should nonetheless avoid saying something that may make them wary of you or refuse to trust you. Alternatively, you can request someone else that they trust unconditionally make the suggestions. By giving them different options about who they could talk to, who could provide treatment, and the treatment options available to them, you can create a source of comfort and have the person decide on their own.

Keep Track of Medication

Expect medication to be part of any treatment plan. You can be helpful by monitoring medication and making sure it is being taken as prescribed and on time. It is not uncommon for a third party, that being you, to inform the doctor if you see side effects, which is often a major reason why people with schizophrenia stop taking their medicines. Take these side-effects seriously and inform the doctor accordingly.

It is usually not easy for a person taking more than one medication to keep track and remember if they have taken their medicine or not. It may also confuse you, but several items can help you, such as pillboxes or timers.

Another crucial point that you need to bear in mind is to make sure that no other drugs or substances are being mixed or taken together, unless prescribed by the same doctor. Even seemingly harmless supplements might not be advised to take.

Be Aware of Relapse

Even if there is an initially promising response to treatments, relapses can happen. Only 10 percent to 20 percent of people diagnosed with schizophrenia do not experience relapses. Most people will experience a gradual return of symptoms over time.

By now, you should have an understanding of the symptoms related to the disorder, such as social withdrawal, insomnia, hallucinations, and the like. However, and more importantly, you should keep an eye on what is known as relapse signatures, which vary from person to person. For one patient, it might be excessive worrying, while for another person it might be them beginning to hear voices.

Knowing these warning signs won't stop a relapse from happening, but it could prevent hospital admission when early treatment is received. While an initial diagnosis of schizophrenia can take to happen, relapses are usually much quicker. You can help the patient by recognizing these symptoms and getting help early before it becomes a full-blown relapse.

Look After Yourself

Although it is crucial that a family member is educated on this disorder and knows how to accommodate the patient, they should never forget to look after themselves in this process. This includes eating properly, resting, avoiding stress, and doing some of the things that they enjoy. Some people often feel guilty when paying attention to themselves, while a loved one is not doing well.

There is no need to view this as a form of selfishness. You cannot help someone else if you are not caring for yourself. Bear in mind, as previously mentioned, that schizophrenia is not curable; it is simply treatable and manageable. Whatever level of support you give your loved one, it has to be a level that can be maintained over the long-term.

It is always hard seeing a loved one go through difficulties, let alone a life-altering medical condition. With the amount of help available for schizophrenia patients as well as their loved ones, you do not have to stand by feeling hopeless and helpless. The more you learn, the more strategies you will be able to develop for yourself to manage a person's symptoms over time.

Chapter 7: Alternative Therapies

People diagnosed with schizophrenia suffer from life-changing symptoms. Their quality of life may be lowered significantly if they don't seek effective treatment. While antipsychotic medication can be very helpful, it can also bring about a variety of unwanted side-effects. This is why scientists are now studying the efficacy of alternative treatments, or at least therapies, that complement the prescribed medications. Over time, many of these new and alternative treatment options may even allow the patient to cut down on their medications, little by little.

Cognitive-Behavioral Therapy

Cognitive therapy is widely used to treat patients with mental illnesses. Talking is the primary feature of this kind of treatment. At first, the therapist will listen carefully to what the affected person has to say and write down every detail to gain an understanding of the patient's life.

The psychiatrist, after analyzing the facts in front of them, will begin to start asking questions. This will include asking about the goals of the patient, and what they hope to gain from treatment.

A good psychiatrist will be skilled in avoiding making patients feel alienated even if the symptoms they exhibit are unique. A key focus of this therapy is identifying the patient's triggers, and the reasons behind them.

A psychiatrist's role in this therapy is to help the schizophrenic person detangle their thoughts, as well as to help them develop healthy coping mechanisms that assist them in avoiding psychotic episodes in the future.

Transcranial Magnetic Stimulation

Transcranial stimulation is the process of directing strong, alternating, magnetic fields towards the scalp to stimulate the cerebral cortex. This is achieved by exciting the neurons and causing activity in the brain that will regulate nerve impulses. This method has been used successfully in the schizophrenic treatment realm when medications fail to control auditory hallucinations.

Fortunately, anesthesia is not required as the procedure is pain-free. Moreover, there are no side-effects except for a mild headache and ear-buzzing because of the sound of the machine.

Very rarely, seizures may occur, but the percentage is too low to really be considered a risk.

Electroconvulsive Therapy

There is no denying that Hollywood has tarnished the reputation and efficacy of electroconvulsive therapy. It is often presented as a torture device used on non-consenting patients. However, this is a myth, and this treatment is highly effective in controlling severe hallucinations, delusions, and catatonia.

That said, it is not painful, as it involves going under general anesthesia to keep the discomfort under control. The procedure involves two electrodes being attached to the patient's scalp, through which the medical professional will send an electrical current, inducing a mild seizure.

Deep Brain Stimulation

Brain stimulation is a more intrusive procedure, but sometimes it is the last resort. It helps in regulating brain chemicals and aiding different lobes in communicating with each other. It involves a pre-scan of the brain by an MRI to determine where to place the electrodes inside the patient's head.

Brain stimulation is a two-stage procedure; the first stage involves planting the electrodes, and it is done while the patient is wide awake because the surgeon needs to examine reactions to know if they are in the right place. The second part of the procedure involves putting the control device near the collarbone. After recovery, the device is programmed and adjusted according to the required voltage. This operation is done with the consent of the patient or their legal guardian, but it should be noted that this is not a completely risk-free treatment.

Side-effects such as seizures, temporary numbness or tingling, and bleeding may deter some from trying this treatment method. However, it should be noted that these side-effects are only temporary, and long-term complications are rather rare.

Creative Therapy

Sometimes having an outlet for negative energy keeps anger under control. This is why advising the patient to join a creative therapy program is a great idea.

There is no pressure to become a great painter or writer for this type of therapy to work. Simply expressing oneself creatively is enough. It has been proven that doodling, for example, can help people to overcome panic attacks. It distracts them from the noise inside their head and effectively quiets their mind.

Ecotherapy

The concept of ecotherapy is to become connected with nature and all it has to offer. Researchers have found that a part of our misery often stems from a detachment from the environment around us.

One ecotherapy method is gardening. The act of soiling, planting seeds, and watering may help distract a person from their daily struggles and help to ground them in reality.

Some programs offer therapy pets to serve as a companion to people with schizophrenia. The unconditional love given by a pet can be a huge help in controlling a person's symptoms.

Yoga

Practicing yoga has been proved useful as a supplementary treatment for schizophrenic individuals. Exercise itself is great, as it releases feel-good hormones into the blood stream that can improve a patient's mood. These endorphins, combined with the calming techniques taught by yoga can be very beneficial in helping a schizophrenic gain control over their moods, emotions, and mental stability.

Supplements

Lack of specific vitamins and nutrients can induce psychosis, depression, and delusions. So, if a person has schizophrenia, it's vital that their nutritional needs are taken care of.

Fish Oil

Some fatty acids, such as those contained in fish oil, can help in reducing inflammation in the brain, which in turn protects the nerves. For that reason, symptoms such as paranoia may lessen, or at least not worsen.

Vitamin B

There are several vitamins that comprise the vitamin B-complex, each carrying its own benefits. For instance, vitamin B6 improves control over jerky movements and reduces restlessness. Some studies suggest that people with schizophrenia may have an anomaly in the gene responsible for metabolizing vitamin B9 (folate). As a result, they tend to be tired, depressed, and socially withdrawn. Vitamin B supplements can help them overcome these symptoms through bypassing the normal metabolizing mechanism and reaching the blood efficiently.

Vitamin E

Side-effects of neuroleptic medications can involve tremors and involuntary movement of eyes, lips, fingers, and arms, which can be both embarrassing and annoying. Fortunately, vitamin E can help to reduce the adverse effects of the drugs and induce stability.

Glycine

It has long been known that low levels of dopamine are common among people with schizophrenia. Glycine deficiency means that the receptor that regulates the release of the "happiness" neurotransmitter is not functioning well. Taking glycine can improve the whole process as it leads to balanced brain chemicals, allowing for better control of one's actions and moods.

Cannabidiol

Marijuana has a lot of derivatives that are now being used in modern medicine. Cannabidiol has anti-anxiety and anti-inflammatory effects that help in sharpening the mind and decreasing delusions. It has also been noted anecdotally that memory improves after consistently ingesting this supplement.

Melatonin

It's no surprise that mentally ill people often have poor sleep. They either sleep too much or suffer from insomnia. When the brain doesn't get to rest, it becomes dysfunctional, and symptoms may develop or worsen. Any treatment plan should include a sleep regulation protocol. This protocol can include taking melatonin, which is a hormone that encourages healthy sleeping cycles.

Chinese Medications

The Chinese have long developed natural medications to help in eliminating some symptoms that schizophrenics may experience. This includes a variety of herbs, animals, and fungi. Although researchers still doubt their efficacy when used alone, using them in addition to mainstream treatment methods can be beneficial.

Stem Cells

The dysfunction of the prefrontal cortex in patients is what leads to the development of psychotic and mental disorders. Utilizing fetal stem cells is the future of science. They are undifferentiated mesenchymal cells that can be stimulated to become differentiated. If interneurons are born and transplanted into the brain, the negative symptoms of schizophrenia may possibly be alleviated, though further studies still need to be conducted.

Immunotherapy

In some clinical studies, doctors have noticed that the immune system plays a role in the development of schizophrenia. Patients usually suffer from abnormalities in the bone marrow and spinal fluid and, in turn, in antibody levels. Immunotherapy using monoclonal antibodies is still under trial for its anti-inflammatory effects on the brain and in reducing paranoia and psychosis.

Conclusion

Those who do not have schizophrenia may have a hard time relating to a lot of thoughts and feelings that go through the schizophrenic mind. While many mental disorders are understood well by the public, schizophrenia is sadly still lagging behind in that department.

The lack of awareness campaigns and public understanding of schizophrenia makes it very challenging for people who suffer or know someone who has schizophrenia. I hope that this book has helped you gain a clearer understanding of this complex disorder, the symptoms that accompany it, as well as how it is diagnosed, and treated.

Unfortunately, there is no cure for schizophrenia, at least not yet. However, many individuals with schizophrenia have achieved an incredible improvement in their symptoms and are able to lead regular lives. Medication, self-help strategies, counseling, and other forms of therapy have netted amazing results across many cases of schizophrenia with varying degrees of severity. It's important to understand that being diagnosed with schizophrenia isn't a death sentence. With a proper diagnosis and treatment plan, most people who have schizophrenia get dramatically better over time.

Many of the challenges of living with schizophrenia are now being gradually reduced, thanks to pharmaceutical advancements and elaborate support systems. In addition to this, scientists and medical professionals are working hard to develop and refine new treatment methods to further support those with schizophrenia.

Remember to never self-diagnose or self-medicate. If after reading this book you believe that you, or a loved one, may have schizophrenia, then I urge you to seek a professional diagnosis. Early diagnosis and a comprehensive treatment plan that encompasses many levels of treatment, including medication, therapy, community support, a healthy diet, supplementation, and exercise will provide you with the highest chances of improvement and a reduction of symptoms.

I would like to thank you for taking the time to read this book and educate yourself on the complex disorder that is schizophrenia. I hope you have found this book to be both informative and helpful, and I wish you the best of luck!

www.ingramcontent.com/pod-product-compliance
Lightning Source LLC
LaVergne TN
LVHW011739060526
838200LV00051B/3247